Lectio Divina

Reading God's

Messages to You

A **MISSION:CHRISTIAN** MEDITATION JOURNAL

Nihil obstat:
Rev. Timothy Hall
Censor librorum
September 4, 2017

Imprimatur:
†Most Rev. John M. Quinn
Bishop of Winona
September 4, 2017

Concept design and development by Jerry Windley-Daoust
Visual design and book build by Steve Nagel
Copy editing by Sibyl Niemann and Karen Lynn Carter

ISBN: 978-1-68192-502-8 (Inventory No. T2391)
LCCN: 2019939983

Printed in the United States of America

Our Sunday Visitor
Huntington, Indiana
www.osv.com

Preface:
God has something to say to you

God wants to speak to you—and what he has to say is so important, it will change your life.

But to hear God's special message for you, you need to listen . . . not just with your ears, but with your whole mind and heart.

Have you ever tried listening to God in prayer? If you have, you may have run into one of these common problems:

- You tried quietly listening for God's voice, but nothing seemed to be happening, so after a minute or two, you gave up.

- Or you found yourself getting distracted by other thoughts . . . like what happened at school earlier in the day, or getting together with friends later, or remembering a scene from your favorite TV show.

- Or you thought you might have "heard" God speaking to you, but you couldn't be sure that the words weren't just your own thoughts.

You might even have wondered why God couldn't just speak to you directly, like he did with some of the people in the Old Testament. You'd probably even settle for a letter!

Well, there's bad news and good news about that.

The bad news is that it's super unlikely that God is going to speak to you "out loud." (Although in rare instances, people do still hear God's words in this way; this phenomenon is known as an *interior locution*.)

The good news is that God *has* written you a sort of "letter inside a letter." This letter to you is "hidden" inside the sacred Scriptures—that is, the Bible.

The Scriptures are God's word for his people, the Church. But he also uses them to speak a special word to every person who seeks him there.

This prayer journal is all about learning to "hear" God speaking to you in the Scriptures using an ancient method developed by the spiritual masters, a method known as *lectio divina*. In the next few pages, you'll get a crash course in *lectio divina*, and then you'll have a chance to practice it yourself.

What is lectio divina?

The words *lectio divina* are Latin for "sacred reading," which is nothing more than reading and then praying over God's word in the Scriptures.

This is a different way of reading than most people are used to. Usually, we read for information or entertainment.

Consider the Scripture passage about Peter and the large catch of fish (Luke 5:1–11). After preaching to the crowds, Jesus gets into Peter's boat and asks him and his friends to throw their nets into the sea: "Put out into the deep water and let down your nets for a catch." Simon is skeptical, but does what Jesus asks. The fishermen end up catching such a large amount of fish, they're left amazed—Simon even falls down at Jesus' feet, saying, "Go away from me, Lord! I am a sinful man!" But Jesus tells him not to be afraid.

There are several ways we could read this passage:

- If we're reading simply for pleasure or entertainment, we might focus on the drama of the story—the surprising and miraculous catch of fish, Peter's reaction, Jesus' response. We might even "enter" the story as if we were there witnessing it.

- Another way to read this passage would be to analyze it for information. We might ask why Jesus wants Peter and his companions to go fishing—isn't that kind of a strange request for a traveling preacher to make? And why does Peter react the way he does?

- A more serious study of the passage would look at what meaning and purpose this story had for the first Christians. Why did they tell this particular story about Jesus, and what did it mean for them?

These are fine ways to read the Scriptures, and in fact, they can be part of the method of *lectio divina*. But *lectio divina* goes beyond these methods to seek what God is saying to *you* inside the passage.

Decoding God's word for you in the Scriptures

Have you ever seen a secret message in a book, a game, or a box of cereal that requires special glasses to decode? To the naked eye, the words are gibberish, but seen through red-colored decoder glasses, the message suddenly becomes clear.

Lectio divina is something like that, but the "decoder" who helps make God's word for us clear is the Holy Spirit.

Unlike other types of writings (school textbooks, poetry, legal codes, mystery novels, and so on), the sacred Scriptures are "inspired" by God. Although the Bible was written down by human authors using their own words, the Holy Spirit "inspired" those authors to write the Scriptures in a way that would communicate what God wanted his people to know for their salvation. The Greek word that the apostle Paul used when he said that "all scripture is inspired by God" (1 Timothy 3:16) is *theopneustos*, or "God-breathed." In other words, God "breathes" his Spirit into the Scriptures.

This makes the Scriptures different from other types of writing. Plato's *Republic* is considered an ancient classic of philosophy, one that contains many important truths. In fact, early Church leaders drew on its insights as they tried to make sense of God's revelation in Jesus. Even so, Plato's *Republic* is not "God-breathed." God's Spirit doesn't live in its words, waiting to speak to the human reader.

At first the writings of the Bible might not seem "alive." They might seem to be ordinary words written by ancient authors for an ancient audience.

But just as that secret message can only be seen with the help of special glasses, the Scriptures take on a new meaning when we read them with the help of the Holy Spirit. This is possible because God breathes his Spirit into us, too, especially through the sacraments: baptism, confirmation, the Eucharist, and so on. (If you haven't been baptized, don't worry—God finds ways to speak to the hearts of all who seek him in the Scriptures.)

The same Spirit who inspired the authors of the Scriptures to write what God wanted to be written for the sake of our salvation also inspires us to understand what God is saying to us in those Scriptures. The Holy Spirit is the "coder" and the "decoder" of the Scriptures.

A way of falling in love

Before we learn about the four steps of praying *lectio divina*, let's step back and check our assumptions about prayer. What do you think prayer is?

We often say that prayer is "talking to God," which it is. But *how* we talk to God makes a big difference! Think about this: Would you rather talk to . . .

. . . your favorite relative, or a super-strict teacher?

. . . your hero (like a sports or music star), or the order-taker at the drive-thru of your favorite fast food place?

. . . your best friend, or a stranger?

The point is, we enjoy talking to some people more than others because we already have a relationship or connection with them. Talking to these people is fun, interesting, and comfortable. Plus, they somehow make us "more." Whether the other person makes us laugh our heads off, or tells interesting stories, or just listens to our feelings with sympathy and understanding, we end up feeling better about ourselves; and in the best relationships, we feel like the other person is an extension of ourselves, another "me."

This is what prayer is like at its best.

People who have this kind of relationship with God enjoy praying. In fact, St. Teresa of Avila, whose teaching on prayer is so widely respected that she is known as a "Doctor of the Church," once told her religious sisters: I know you want to stay up all night praying, but be sure to get some sleep!

Another Doctor of the Church, St. Thérèse of Lisieux, said this about prayer:

> For me, prayer is a surge of the heart;
> it is a simple look turned toward heaven,
> it is a cry of recognition and of love.

If it sounds like Thérèse was "in love" with God, she would certainly agree with you. At its best, prayer is like being "in love." Many spiritual writers use romantic language to talk about their relationships with God; others speak of the kind of love that a child has for a beloved parent.

Unfortunately, for many people, prayer is nothing more than some memorized words that we're supposed to say at certain times, like before a meal or at bedtime, or at Mass. For them, prayer is like talking to that super-strict teacher: you say what you have to and no more. For other people, prayer is like talking to the order-taker at a fast food joint—it's something to do when they want or need something. And for a lot of people, prayer is just plain awkward, because God is like a stranger to them.

Lectio divina is one of many ways of praying that aim to move us from that awkward, uncomfortable prayer—the kind that we don't like to do and never seem to have time to do—toward prayer that we look forward to doing because we have a deep friendship with God.

This is the goal of *lectio divina*, but it doesn't happen overnight, any more than two people really fall in love overnight. It is a gradual process . . . one that begins with reading God's "love letters" to us.

6

The steps of lectio divina

Lectio divina is a very ancient prayer tradition. The earliest Christians were Jews who were very used to praying with Scripture. St. Benedict of Nursia (480–543) was the first to use the term *lectio divina* ("sacred reading") when he included it in the rule of life for all of his monks. Other spiritual masters such as St. Bernard of Clairvaux, Guigo the Angelic, and St. John of the Cross continued to develop the practice over the centuries, until it reached the form most people know today.

It was Guigo, a Carthusian monk, who first set out the four steps or movements of *lectio divina*. Here they are, with their Latin names in parenthesis:

- **Reading *(lectio)*** In the first step, you choose a reading, and you read it several times, leaving room for the Holy Spirit to call your attention to a word, phrase, or line that God wants you to hear.

- **Meditation *(meditatio)*** In the meditation step, you think about the word or words that the Holy Spirit has called to your attention, holding them in your mind and considering them from different angles.

- **Prayer *(oratio)*** In the prayer step, you respond to the sacred words in prayer, either silently or out loud, or in writing.

- **Contemplation *(contemplatio)*** In the contemplation step, you rest in God's presence, quieting yourself and listening for God's response to your prayer.

Even though we've outlined four movements or "steps" to *lectio divina*, it's important to know that your prayer might not follow the steps exactly. *Lectio divina* is not like changing a car tire or making a cake, where the order of the steps is critical to success. It's more like a deep conversation with a friend.

Although *lectio divina* always begins with reading, and often progresses naturally through the next few steps, you might find yourself bouncing around a bit. For example, you might read the text and have an immediate reaction that you voice to God (the prayer step); then, you might pause and think about the words more (the meditation step); then, if you find your mind drifting, you might go back and re-read the text again. After a while, you might move into contemplation . . . or you might not, and that would be okay.

An example using Psalm 23

Let's try out each of the steps. For a text, we'll choose Psalm 23:

The Lord is my shepherd, I shall not want.
    He makes me lie down in green pastures;
he leads me beside still waters;
    he restores my soul.

He leads me in right paths
    for his name's sake.
Even though I walk through the darkest valley,
    I fear no evil;
for you are with me;
    your rod and your staff—
    they comfort me.

You prepare a table before me
    in the presence of my enemies;
you anoint my head with oil;
    my cup overflows.

Surely goodness and mercy shall follow me
    all the days of my life,
and I shall dwell in the house of the Lord
    my whole life long.

Before you begin

Before beginning *lectio divina*, you might want to prepare yourself for encountering God:

- **Find a quiet place that is free from distractions.**

- **If you like, light a candle and place a crucifix or other holy image where you can see it.**

- **Sit, stand, or kneel with good posture.**

- Relax the muscles of your face and body, and relax your breathing.

- Quiet yourself down. Pray:

Let us remember that we are in the holy presence of God.

or:

O God, come to my assistance; Lord, make haste to help me.

- Spend a few moments in silence.

You don't need to do these things before beginning *lectio*; in theory, you can pray anywhere, at any time. But most people find it easier to do so in a quiet environment after some preparation.

Reading

Begin by choosing a text. You'll find a list of possible texts in the back of this journal (page 54). Some other options include:

- Flipping through the Bible until you find something that strikes you.

- Using one of the Mass readings for the day.

- Using one of the readings for the Liturgy of the Hours for the day.

- Working your way through the Bible in a methodical way, following a Bible study or another program for reading the Bible.

(If you want to use the day's readings for Mass, you can find them at the website of the U.S. Catholic bishops, usccb.org; click on Daily Readings. Many Catholic smartphone apps also include the daily readings, as well as readings for the Liturgy of the Hours.)

Read the text a few times, either silently or out loud. You might even find it helpful to copy the text down.

Most of us are in the habit of reading quickly, skimming the words for their basic meaning. When you do sacred reading, however, you want to slow down. Pause between words, or at the end of key phrases, leaving room for the Holy Spirit to work in you.

Read the text several times in this way. What word, phrase, or line stands out to you? What "speaks" to you? The Holy Spirit may draw your attention to the words in different ways. Sometimes, you might feel a strong emotional response (positive or negative). Other times, you might read a phrase that startles you, or that seems to speak directly to a problem in your life.

Try It: Take a moment right now to read Psalm 23 in this way, and write down the word, phrase, or line that the Holy Spirit seems to be placing on your heart.

_____

_____

_____

_____

Meditation

Once you have identified your sacred reading, move on to the meditation step. In this step, you will seek God in the words of the text.

It is _seeking God_ that makes meditation more than academic study or daydreaming. In meditation, our goal is not to understand, grasp, or "master" the words we're reading, but to use them as a doorway through which we pass in order to meet God.

"Careful listening" is one way of describing this moment in _lectio divina_. Imagine you're trying to hear a faint sound in order to find its source: a bird in the woods, a cricket in the grass, or even your missing cell phone in your house. You tilt your head this way and that, and you become very still, focusing your whole self on the sound. Meditation can be like that, except we listen to the "sound" of the words in order to find their source, which is God.

The spiritual masters often use the image of "eating" the words of the text to describe the meditation step. They talk about "savoring" or even "chewing" the words.

How you do this is up to you. Let's say you've chosen the words, "I fear no evil; for you are with me." You might look intently at those words. You might trace them with your fingertips, or silently mouth the words over and over, letting them sink into your heart.

Or perhaps the words in your heart are "still waters." You might imagine those still waters . . . maybe you'll even immerse yourself in them! Similarly, if the words are, "The Lord is my shepherd," then you might imagine yourself in the company of God, personified as a shepherd.

During your time of meditation, you might consider one or more of these questions:

- How do the words make you feel? Comforted? Disturbed? Joyful? Confused?

- Why did these words come to your attention?

- Do they speak to anything that is happening in your life right now?

- Is God trying to say something to you? What is he calling you to do?

Take some time now to meditate on your sacred words from Psalms 23.

If you find your mind wandering, don't worry—it's a common experience, especially if you're just getting started with this type of prayer, or haven't had enough quiet "down time" recently. Simply return to the reading step, re-reading the text, or repeating it silently on your lips.

You might also think about whether the "distraction" is actually something God wants you to bring to prayer. If you can't stop thinking about the fight you had with your friend, for instance, then bring that concern to God in prayer.

Try It: After you are done with this step, answer one or more of the questions above.

_____

_____

_____

_____

Prayer

If the meditation step is all about listening, then this next step—prayer (or in Latin, *oratio*)—is about responding to what we "heard" during our meditation.

St. Theresa of Avila once described meditation as a conversation between friends "in secret." This isn't exactly the type of lighthearted joking you have with your friends at lunch. Your conversation with God *could* be lighthearted; in fact, you might be most comfortable beginning your prayer with some humor. But God is also calling you to something deeper: a sharing of hearts.

In the conversation of *lectio divina*, God opens his heart to you in his word, and calls you to respond by sharing the "secrets" of your own heart: those thoughts, desires, and feelings that you hide from everyone—even yourself. God knows what is in your heart already (probably better than you do!). But think about what happens when a friend chooses to share a secret about herself with you. How does it change your relationship? That act of trust strengthens the bonds of friendship, and it is the same way with God.

Depending on what you "heard" in the meditation step, your prayer could take many different forms:

- If God spoke to you in a special way, you might offer thanks: "Thank you, Lord, for sharing your love for me!"

- If you found the reading difficult or confusing, you could ask God for guidance and clarity: "What are you trying to say to me, Lord? Open my heart!"

- If the reading left you feeling angry, afraid, or overwhelmed, you could bring that to prayer, too: "God, I'm scared by what you're asking me to do here; could you, please, offer some reassurance?"

Any conversation is a back-and-forth exchange. Moving freely between the reading, meditation, and prayer steps is perfectly natural! You might offer some words of prayer, then pause to "listen" again by meditating on the reading some more.

Try It: Take some time now to pray in response to the text you choose from Psalm 23. You might want to speak your prayer out loud, or write it below. Or use the writing space to summarize your experience in this step.

Contemplation

At some point during *lectio divina*, you may find that all the words pass away. You're not speaking to God, and God is not speaking to you—not with words, at least. Instead, you experience a strong sense of God's presence. You might experience this in one or more of the following ways:

- A strong surge of love for God welling up within you.

- God's love completely enveloping you.

- An overwhelming sense of peace.

- A strong desire for God—almost a spiritual "thirst."

- A sense of the physical boundaries of your body passing away as you "lose" yourself in God.

- Brightness, or waves of light.

- A feeling of warmth or tingling passing over your body.

What's going on? You may be experiencing the presence of God. If so, you have moved into the final step of *lectio divina*, contemplation. If meditation is a doorway to God's presence, contemplation is passing through that doorway into that presence; it is an intimate communion with the Lord.

The most basic feature of contemplation is that words are replaced by a simple feeling—the "surge of the heart" and "cry of love" described by St. Thérèse of Lisieux. Other spiritual masters have described contemplative prayer in similar ways:

- St. Theophan the Recluse: "Whoever has passed through actions and thought to true feeling will pray without words, for God is God of the heart."

- St. Padre Pio of Pietrelcina: "You must speak to Jesus also with the heart, besides with the lips; indeed, in certain cases you must speak to him only with the heart."

- St. Bonaventure: "When we pray, the voice of the heart must be heard more than proceedings from the mouth."

In her autobiography, St. Teresa of Avila described the experience of contemplation in this way:

> When picturing Christ in the way I have mentioned, or sometimes even when reading, I used unexpectedly to experience a consciousness of the presence of God, of such a kind that I could not possibly doubt that he was within me or that I was wholly engulfed in him. This was in no sense a vision. . . . The soul is suspended in such a way that it seems to be completely outside itself. The will loves; the memory, I think, is almost lost; while the understanding, I believe, though it is not lost, does not reason—I mean that it does not work, but is amazed at the extent of all it can understand; for God wills it to realize that it understands nothing of what his majesty represents to it.
>
> This is . . . entirely the gift of God.

Contemplation *is* a gift; it's not something we can make happen, or achieve, although approaching *lectio divina* with an open heart and spending good time on the first three steps prepares the way for contemplative prayer.

It's also important to note that people have different experiences of contemplation. Prayer is a personal relationship, after all, and every relationship is unique. God will come to you in whatever way works best for your unique relationship.

Try It: As part of your "practice" with Psalm 23, take time now to simply "rest in the presence of the Lord." Write about your experience in the space below.

_____

_____

_____

After your prayer

When the time you have set out to pray is over, or when the Holy Spirit moves you to finish, make the Sign of the Cross.

As you practice *lectio divina* in this journal, take time after each experience to record how it went. By writing down your thoughts, you may realize things that will help you do better next time. You will also have a record of your progress in prayer.

Do that now in the space below.

_____

_____

_____

_____

_____

Problems praying

The *Catechism of the Catholic Church* includes an entire section titled, "The Battle of Prayer" (#2725–2745) that talks about some of the problems people typically encounter in prayer: distraction, dryness, discouragement, and so on.

Such problems in prayer are common; even saints and superheroes of the spiritual life experience them, and the writings of the Church's spiritual masters are filled with pages and pages of advice about how to handle them.

The *Catechism* offers three main suggestions for combatting these problems:

- **Humility**. If we think we don't need God, prayer will be difficult—even impossible. Masters of prayer recognize that they *need* God, not just a little bit, or when things get tough, but entirely, like a little baby needs its mother. They also recognize that they need the help of the Holy Spirit in order to pray well. A simple prayer of humility is: "Lord, I don't know how to pray. Please inspire me!"

- **Trust**. Sometimes, we feel that our prayer is not heard or answered. Or we feel that God is not present. We can respond to these feelings with trust that God wants our happiness and well-being. Our trust is based not only on our own previous experience of God, but on what he has done for his people throughout history, especially in Jesus Christ.

- **Perseverance**. Perseverance means sticking with prayer, even when it feels fruitless or unrewarding. The masters of prayer tell us that if we keep praying no matter how we feel about it, eventually it will become easier.

Like everything else worth doing in life, prayer requires a commitment of our time, energy, and effort. No one becomes a great artist, a great athlete, or a great scientist without lots of practice (and lots of mistakes along the way!). Two people don't become really good friends without spending lots of time together.

It's the same way with prayer. But as untold thousands of people have attested, the effort is worth it! Getting to know God heart-to-heart will fill your heart with good things—and change your life.

Practicing lectio divina

In the following pages, you'll find

- seven texts for practicing *lectio divina*,

- plus seven blank prayer journal entries for texts of your own choosing. Each entry contains writing space for journaling the steps of *lectio divina*.

The prayer of *lectio divina* is not usually written down; normally, it is done silently, individually or in groups. However, there are some advantages to journaling your *lectio divina* experience, especially as you get started. Some people find that they pray better when they write their prayer because it helps them focus, and opens up new possibilities. But even if that isn't your experience, writing your prayer experience will help you think about how it's going, and how you can improve. It will also provide you with a record of your prayer experience for you to look back on later. And if you're doing this journal as part of a group, your writing might help you discuss your experience with others.

If you're not the writing type, no worries! Jot down words or phrases, or even doodle little icons or pictures, if you find that helpful. God knows your heart . . . and doesn't grade for grammar and spelling!

Reading 1: Seek the Lord

Isaiah 55:6–11

This passage from the prophet Isaiah encourages the people of Israel to turn back to God . . . and reassures them that God's promise to them will come true.

Seek the Lord while he may be found,
    call upon him while he is near.
Let the wicked forsake their way,
    and sinners their thoughts;
Let them turn to the Lord to find mercy;
    to our God, who is generous in forgiving.
For my thoughts are not your thoughts,
    nor are your ways my ways—oracle of the Lord.
For as the heavens are higher than the earth,
    so are my ways higher than your ways,
    my thoughts higher than your thoughts.

Yet just as from the heavens
    the rain and snow come down
And do not return there
    till they have watered the earth,
    making it fertile and fruitful,
Giving seed to the one who sows
    and bread to the one who eats,
So shall my word be
    that goes forth from my mouth;
It shall not return to me empty,
    but shall do what pleases me,
    achieving the end for which I sent it.

Seek the Lord

● Read

Read the text a few times, either silently or out loud. Remember: slow down. Pause between words, or at the end of key phrases, leaving room for the Holy Spirit to work in you. What word, phrase, or line stands out to you? What "speaks" to you? Write down the words that the Holy Spirit seems to be placing on your heart.

_____

_____

_____

● Meditate

Seek God in the words you chose from your reading. Savor the words, listening carefully for God's voice in them. Reflect on these questions:

- How do the words make you feel?

- Why did these words come to your attention?

- Is God trying to say something to you?

- Write down some of the thoughts you have during your time of meditation, either now (if you find that helpful) or after you are done praying.

_____

_____

_____

_____

_____

_____

_____

Pray

Take some time now to pray in response to God's word to you. Write your prayer below. Or use the space to summarize your experience in this step.

_____

_____

_____

_____

_____

_____

_____

_____

_____

Contemplate

Rest in God's loving presence, listening for his response to your prayer. Afterward, record your experience with this step in the space below.

_____

_____

_____

_____

_____

_____

_____

Record your experience

After you are finished praying with this sacred reading, take some time to record your experience. Some questions to consider:

- How long did your prayer last?

- How did you feel when you began, and how did you feel when you finished?

- What was good, and what was challenging?

- How did this sacred reading affect your relationship with God, or the way you understand yourself?

Reading 2: Exodus from Slavery to Freedom

Exodus 14:10–14

The Exodus is the oldest story in the Bible. It relates how God freed his people, the Israelites, from slavery in Egypt, and led them to a new land—one "flowing with milk and honey." This text picks up the story as the Israelites appear to be trapped between the pursuing Egyptian army and the Red Sea.

Now Pharaoh was near when the Israelites looked up and saw that the Egyptians had set out after them. Greatly frightened, the Israelites cried out to the Lord. To Moses they said, "Were there no burial places in Egypt that you brought us to die in the wilderness? What have you done to us, bringing us out of Egypt? Did we not tell you this in Egypt, when we said, 'Leave us alone that we may serve the Egyptians'? Far better for us to serve the Egyptians than to die in the wilderness." But Moses answered the people, "Do not fear! Stand your ground and see the victory the Lord will win for you today. For these Egyptians whom you see today you will never see again. The Lord will fight for you; you have only to keep still."

Exodus from Slavery to Freedom

● **Read:** *If you need a refresher on the steps, refer to pages 18–19.*

_____

_____

_____

● **Meditate**

_____

_____

_____

_____

_____

_____

● **Pray**

_____

_____

_____

_____

_____

_____

Contemplate

Record your experience

Reading 3: True Friendship

Ben Sira 6:5–17

This reading is taken from the Book of Ben Sira (also known as Sirach or Ecclesiasticus), one of the Bible's books of wisdom. (This book is omitted from many Protestant versions of the Bible.) It is written in the style of a father's advice to his son.

Pleasant speech multiplies friends,
    and gracious lips, friendly greetings.
Let those who are friendly to you be many,
    but one in a thousand your confidant.
When you gain friends, gain them through testing,
    and do not be quick to trust them.
For there are friends when it suits them,
    but they will not be around in time of trouble.
Another is a friend who turns into an enemy,
    and tells of the quarrel to your disgrace.
Others are friends, table companions,
    but they cannot be found in time of affliction.
When things go well, they are your other self,
    and lord it over your servants.
If disaster comes upon you, they turn against you
    and hide themselves.
Stay away from your enemies,
    and be on guard with your friends.
Faithful friends are a sturdy shelter;
    whoever finds one finds a treasure.
Faithful friends are beyond price,
    no amount can balance their worth.
Faithful friends are life-saving medicine;
    those who fear God will find them.
Those who fear the Lord enjoy stable friendship,
    for as they are, so will their neighbors be.

Read: *If you need a refresher on the steps, refer to pages 18–19.*

_____

_____

_____

Meditate

_____

_____

_____

_____

_____

_____

_____

Pray

_____

_____

_____

_____

_____

_____

_____

True Friendship

_____
_____
_____
_____
_____
_____
_____
_____

Contemplate

_____
_____
_____
_____
_____

Record your experience

_____
_____
_____

Reading 4: Mary's song

Luke 1:46–56

Mary sings this hymn of praise after she and Elizabeth, an older relative, exchange greetings. Both women are miraculously pregnant with special children: Mary, with the Son of God; and Elizabeth, with John the Baptist. Mary's song reflects her joy at being able to participate in God's plan of salvation. Since Mary is the model Christian and the mother of the Church, her song is our song, too.

And Mary said,

"My soul magnifies the Lord,
    and my spirit rejoices in God my Savior,
for he has looked with favor on the lowliness of his servant.
    Surely, from now on all generations will call me blessed;
for the Mighty One has done great things for me,
    and holy is his name.
His mercy is for those who fear him
    from generation to generation.
He has shown strength with his arm;
    he has scattered the proud in the thoughts of their hearts.
He has brought down the powerful from their thrones,
    and lifted up the lowly;
he has filled the hungry with good things,
    and sent the rich away empty.
He has helped his servant Israel,
    in remembrance of his mercy,
according to the promise he made to our ancestors,
    to Abraham and to his descendants forever."

And Mary remained with her about three months and then returned to her home.

Mary's Song

● **Read:** *If you need a refresher on the steps, refer to pages 18–19.*

_____

_____

_____

● **Meditate**

_____

_____

_____

_____

_____

_____

_____

● **Pray**

_____

_____

_____

_____

_____

_____

_____

_____

_____

_____

_____

_____

_____

_____

Contemplate

_____

_____

_____

_____

_____

Record your experience

_____

_____

_____

_____

Reading 5: Bartimaeus meets Jesus

Mark 10:46–52

This is one of several stories in the Gospel about Jesus healing the blind. Blindness can also be a metaphor for not being able to see or understand spiritual truths.

They came to Jericho. And as he was leaving Jericho with his disciples and a sizable crowd, Bartimaeus, a blind man, the son of Timaeus, sat by the roadside begging. On hearing that it was Jesus of Nazareth, he began to cry out and say, "Jesus, son of David, have pity on me." And many rebuked him, telling him to be silent. But he kept calling out all the more, "Son of David, have pity on me." Jesus stopped and said, "Call him." So they called the blind man, saying to him, "Take courage; get up, he is calling you." He threw aside his cloak, sprang up, and came to Jesus. Jesus said to him in reply, "What do you want me to do for you?" The blind man replied to him, "Master, I want to see." Jesus told him, "Go your way; your faith has saved you." Immediately he received his sight and followed him on the way.

Read: *If you need a refresher on the steps, refer to pages 18–19.*

_____

_____

_____

Meditate

_____

_____

_____

_____

_____

_____

Pray

_____

_____

_____

_____

_____

_____

_____

Bartimaeus meets Jesus

● *Contemplate*

Record your experience

Reading 6: Depend on God

Matthew 6:25–39

This passage is from the Sermon on the Mount (Matthew chapters 5—7), a collection of teachings. After teaching about almsgiving and generosity, Jesus urges his followers to depend on God for their needs.

"Therefore I tell you, do not worry about your life, what you will eat [or drink], or about your body, what you will wear. Is not life more than food and the body more than clothing? Look at the birds in the sky; they do not sow or reap, they gather nothing into barns, yet your heavenly Father feeds them. Are not you more important than they? Can any of you by worrying add a single moment to your life-span? Why are you anxious about clothes? Learn from the way the wild flowers grow. They do not work or spin. But I tell you that not even Solomon in all his splendor was clothed like one of them. If God so clothes the grass of the field, which grows today and is thrown into the oven tomorrow, will he not much more provide for you, O you of little faith? So do not worry and say, 'What are we to eat?' or 'What are we to drink?' or 'What are we to wear?' All these things the pagans seek. Your heavenly Father knows that you need them all. But seek first the kingdom [of God] and his righteousness, and all these things will be given you besides. Do not worry about tomorrow; tomorrow will take care of itself. Sufficient for a day is its own evil."

Depend on God

● **Read:** *If you need a refresher on the steps, refer to pages 18–19.*

_____

_____

_____

● **Meditate**

_____

_____

_____

_____

_____

_____

_____

● **Pray**

_____

_____

_____

_____

_____

_____

_____

_____

_____

_____

_____

_____

_____

_____

_____

Contemplate

_____

_____

_____

_____

_____

_____

Record your experience

_____

_____

_____

_____

Reading 7: Love

1 Corinthians 13:1–13

This is from the letter of Paul to the church he established in the city of Corinth. This reading is part of a longer section of the letter dealing with the various gifts that the Holy Spirit distributes to people for the sake of the Church. Here, he says that none of these other gifts are worth anything without love.

If I speak in the tongues of mortals and of angels, but do not have love, I am a noisy gong or a clanging cymbal. And if I have prophetic powers, and understand all mysteries and all knowledge, and if I have all faith, so as to remove mountains, but do not have love, I am nothing. If I give away all my possessions, and if I hand over my body so that I may boast, but do not have love, I gain nothing.

Love is patient; love is kind; love is not envious or boastful or arrogant or rude. It does not insist on its own way; it is not irritable or resentful; it does not rejoice in wrongdoing, but rejoices in the truth. It bears all things, believes all things, hopes all things, endures all things.

Love never ends. But as for prophecies, they will come to an end; as for tongues, they will cease; as for knowledge, it will come to an end. For we know only in part, and we prophesy only in part; but when the complete comes, the partial will come to an end. When I was a child, I spoke like a child, I thought like a child, I reasoned like a child; when I became an adult, I put an end to childish ways. For now we see in a mirror, dimly, but then we will see face to face. Now I know only in part; then I will know fully, even as I have been fully known. And now faith, hope, and love abide, these three; and the greatest of these is love.

Read: *If you need a refresher on the steps, refer to pages 18–19.*

_____

_____

_____

Meditate

_____

_____

_____

_____

_____

_____

_____

Pray

_____

_____

_____

_____

_____

_____

_____

Love

_____

_____

_____

_____

_____

_____

_____

_____

_____

● Contemplate

_____

_____

_____

_____

_____

_____

_____

Record your experience

_____

_____

_____

_____

_____

Reading 8 *If you need a refresher on the steps, refer to pages 18–19.*

The text: *Choose a sacred text from the list on pages 54–55.*

● **Read**

● **Meditate**

● **Pray**

_____

_____

_____

_____

_____

_____

_____

_____

Contemplate

_____

_____

_____

_____

_____

_____

Record your experience

_____

_____

_____

_____

_____

Reading 9 *If you need a refresher on the steps, refer to pages 18–19.*

The text: Choose a sacred text from the list on pages 54–55.

_____

● **Read**

_____

_____

_____

● **Meditate**

_____

_____

_____

_____

_____

_____

_____

● **Pray**

_____

_____

_____

_____

Contemplate

Record your experience

Reading 10 *If you need a refresher on the steps, refer to pages 18–19.*

The text: *Choose a sacred text from the list on pages 54–55.*

_____

● **Read**

_____

_____

_____

● **Meditate**

_____

_____

_____

_____

_____

_____

● **Pray**

_____

_____

_____

_____

Contemplate

Record your experience

Reading 11 *If you need a refresher on the steps, refer to pages 18–19.*

The text: *Choose a sacred text from the list on pages 54–55.*

_____

● **Read**

_____

_____

_____

● **Meditate**

_____

_____

_____

_____

_____

_____

_____

● **Pray**

_____

_____

_____

_____

_____

_____

_____

_____

_____

_____

_____

_____

_____

Contemplate

_____

_____

_____

_____

_____

Record your experience

_____

_____

_____

_____

Reading 12 *If you need a refresher on the steps, refer to pages 18–19.*

The text: *Choose a sacred text from the list on pages 54–55.*

_____

● Read

_____
_____
_____

● Meditate

_____
_____
_____
_____
_____
_____

● Pray

_____
_____
_____
_____

Contemplate

Record your experience

Reading 13 *If you need a refresher on the steps, refer to pages 18–19.*

The text: *Choose a sacred text from the list on pages 54–55.*

_____

● **Read**

_____

_____

_____

● **Meditate**

_____

_____

_____

_____

_____

_____

_____

● **Pray**

_____

_____

_____

_____

Contemplate

Record your experience

Reading 14 *If you need a refresher on the steps, refer to pages 18–19.*

The text: *Choose a sacred text from the list on pages 54–55.*

_____

● **Read**

_____

_____

_____

● **Meditate**

_____

_____

_____

_____

_____

_____

● **Pray**

_____

_____

_____

_____

Contemplate

Record your experience

Additional scriptures for lectio divina

1 Samuel 3:1–10 (The call of Samuel)
Now the Lord came and stood there, calling as before, "Samuel! Samuel!" And Samuel said, "Speak, for your servant is listening."

Psalm 8 (Divine majesty and human dignity)
. . . what are human beings that you are mindful of them, / mortals that you care for them?

Psalm 43:3–5 (Hope in the Lord)
O send out your light and your truth / let them lead me . . .

Psalm 130 (Waiting for divine rescue)
Out of the depths I cry to you, O Lord.

Isaiah 43:2–7 (The Lord will save)
. . . you are precious in my sight / and honored, and I love you . . .

Matthew 5:13–16 (Salt and light)
"You are the light of the world."

Matthew 5:43–48 (Love of enemies)
"But I say to you, Love your enemies and pray for those who persecute you."

Matthew 7:7–11 (Ask, seek, knock)
"Ask, and it will be given you."

Matthew 14:14–21 (Jesus feeds five thousand)
And all ate and were filled. . . .

Matthew 14:22–33 (Jesus invites Peter to walk on water)
Peter answered him, "Lord, if it is you, command me to come to you on the water."

Mark 1:14–15 (The proclamation of the kingdom)
Now after John was arrested, Jesus came to Galilee, proclaiming the good news of God, and saying, "The time is fulfilled, and the kingdom of God has come near; repent, and believe in the good news."

Mark 2:1–12 (Healing of the paralytic)
"I say to you, stand up, take your mat and go to your home."

Mark 10:13–16 (Jesus blesses the children)
"Truly I tell you, whoever does not receive the kingdom of God as a little child will never enter it."

Mark 15:6–20 (The scourging and mocking of Jesus)
They shouted back, "Crucify him!"

Mark 15:21–39 (The Crucifixion)
Jesus cried out with a loud voice, "Eloi, Eloi, lema sabachthani?" which means, "My God, my God, why have you forsaken me?"

Luke 1:26–38 (The Annunciation)
The angel said to her, "Do not be afraid, Mary, for you have found favor with God."

Luke 2:8–20 (The Annunciation to the shepherds)
But the angel said to them, "Do not be afraid; for see—I am bringing you good news of great joy for all the people. . . ."

Luke 2:41–52 (The boy Jesus in the temple)
When his parents saw him they were astonished; and his mother said to him, "Child, why have you treated us like this?"

Luke 4:1–13 (Jesus is tempted in the desert)
Jesus, full of the Holy Spirit, returned from the Jordan and was led by the Spirit in the wilderness. . . .

Luke 5:1–11 (Jesus calls the first disciples)
When he had finished speaking, he said to Simon, "Put out into the deep water and let down your nets for a catch."

Luke 8:22–25 (Jesus calms the stormy sea)
A windstorm swept down on the lake, and the boat was filling with water, and they were in danger.

Luke 6:27–36 (Love of enemies)
Be merciful, just as your Father is merciful.

Luke 10:25–37 (Parable of the Good Samaritan)
"Which of these three, do you think, was a neighbor to the man who fell into the hands of the robbers?"

Luke 10:38–42 (Mary and Martha)
"Lord, do you not care that my sister has left me to do all the work by myself? Tell her then to help me."

John 2:1–12 (The wedding at Cana)
His mother said to the servants, "Do whatever he tells you."

Philippians 1:6 (The work of the Holy Spirit)
I am confident of this, that the one who began a good work among you will bring it to completion by the day of Jesus Christ.

Ephesians 2:8–10 (Saved by faith)
For we are what he has made us . . .